Quiet Spaces

The brf prayer and spirituality journal

Bread for the journey

Edited by Heather Fenton

Published by
The Bible Reading Fellowship
15 The Chambers
Abingdon, OX14 3FE
United Kingdom
Tel: +44 (0)1865 319700
Email: enquiries@brf.org.uk
Website: www.brf.org.uk
BRF is a Registered Charity

ISBN 978 1 84101 830 0
First published 2011
10 9 8 7 6 5 4 3 2 1 0

Acknowledgements
Scripture quotations taken from The Holy Bible, New International Version, copyright © 1973, 1978, 1984 by International Bible Society, are used by permission of Hodder & Stoughton, a member of the Hachette Livre UK Group. All rights reserved. 'NIV' is a registered trademark of International Bible Society. UK trademark number 1448790.

Scripture quotations taken from The New Revised Standard Version of the Bible, Anglicised Edition, copyright © 1989, 1995 by the Division of Christian Education of the National Council of the Churches of Christ in the USA, and are used by permission. All rights reserved.

Extracts from the Authorised Version of the Bible (The King James Bible), the rights in which are vested in the Crown, are reproduced by permission of the Crown's patentee, Cambridge University Press.

Taken from the New Jerusalem Bible, published and copyright © 1985 by Darton, Longman and Todd Ltd and les Editions du Cerf, and by Doubleday, a division of Bantam Doubleday Dell Publishing Group, Inc. Used by permission of Darton, Longman and Todd Ltd, and Doubleday, a division of Random House, Inc.

Taken from the New Jerusalem Bible, published and copyright © 1985 by Darton, Longman and Todd Ltd and les Editions du Cerf, and by Doubleday, a division of Bantam Doubleday Dell Publishing Group, Inc. Used by permission of Darton, Longman and Todd Ltd, and Doubleday, a division of Random House, Inc.

A catalogue record for this book is available from the British Library

Printed in the UK by Harcourt Litho

Contents

VOLUME 19

The Editor writes...

Heather Fenton is the Editor of *Quiet Spaces*.

Thanks for joining us at our meal! This time round we are tasting some good food of the word of God, and our focus will be on bread. What a feast we have in store for you!

Among the good things set out on the table is Tom's exploration of Jesus calling himself 'the bread of life', which is one of the 'I am' phrases found in John's Gospel. As Tom helps us to think about who Jesus is, elsewhere I enable us to think about 'Bethlehem: the house of bread'—the 'house of bread' is the meaning of the name of the place from which the bread of life comes. Meanwhile bread is one of Margaret's favourite sections of the supermarket shelves, stacked with a wonderful selection. Sometimes she buys it straight off the shelves but she also likes making her own, and she tells us how to make some, and what meditations we can draw out from doing this.

Tim Blewitt writes for us under the intriguing heading 'Entertaining angels'—entertaining angels without knowing it. Furthermore David Winter tells us about *lectio divina* or spiritual reading, which and more and more people today are discovering as a fresh and inspirational way to approach the sacred text, which in turn makes possible a radically different, though not contradictory, approach to scripture.

If you want to have a quiet time or a whole day of quiet with a group of people, why not try incorporating the 'bread time' liturgy, and afterwards you could serve some Irish Soda farls (yum!), made according to the *Quiet Spaces* recipe! (Is this the first recipe to appear in *Quiet Spaces*, I ask myself?)

Until the advent of television, microwaveable meals and similar supposed 'improvements' to our daily lives, eating was a very sociable activity. It also took up a lot of time and was therefore seen as something much more important than we may view it today. Especially at times when it was scarce, food had to be treated with great respect. Alexander Carmichael, who was born just before Queen Victoria came to the throne, is known for his attempts to collect ancient Gaelic prayers. Many of these are about food, or things related to food, and made me think about how we could weave a pattern of thanksgiving for various aspects of food into our own hectic lives.

Talking of food reminds me of the ancient festival of Lammas, and the article 'Give us this day our daily bread' helps us to think about how we have developed the basic idea of bread over many generations and suggests some ways in which we might recognise and celebrate this.

Most of the food I have mentioned so far is, of course, bread, a basic staple in the West. The apple is a very popular fruit here in Britain, however, and I remember hearing the choir of Ludlow church singing 'Jesus Christ the apple tree' there a couple of years ago. So you too can discover this old song, to bite into and to enjoy.

Margaret's space reflects on 'food for the journey', and John's prayers, which combine 'daily bread' and 'bread of life', add to the rich meal prepared for you. Breakfast is said by many to be the most important meal of the day, but Tony Horsfall helps us to think about the quiet time as an important 'meal time' and makes some suggestions for a practical recipe for doing this.

So recipes, ideas, worship material and new insights are all here encouraging you in your own journey, and giving us the strength to go on, discovering abundant food for the journey and, above all, realising again that Jesus is indeed the 'living bread that came down from heaven' (John 6:51, NIV).

MARGARET HARVEY

Bread

BREAD. It is my favourite section of the supermarket shelves, stacked with a wonderful selection of different kinds of bread. There are loaves of all shapes and sizes reflecting countries and traditions from around the world. From the in-store bakery wafts that reassuring smell redolent of security and warmth. But none of it tastes or smells like bread cooked in our own kitchen. My loaves may not look as professional but there is something very satisfying about a loaf of bread one has produced oneself.

... a basis for a very
practical meditation

Making bread links us with people and places. I know, as I put out the ingredients together, that people in many countries have been doing something similar for thousands of years. A millstone used for grinding corn has been found that is thought to be 7500 years old. Loaves and rolls have been found in ancient Egyptian tombs, and the British Museum's Egyptian gallery has a loaf baked around 1500BC.

The process of bread making can become a basis for a very practical meditation. If you use a bread maker, as I usually do, try making this loaf completely by hand. Set aside some time to feel, think, smell, pray, taste, listen.

author

Margaret Harvey is a retired priest in the Church in Wales. She has been running Coeg y Groes Retreat House. Margaret writes a regular column in *Quiet Spaces*.

First, assemble the ingredients. Here is a basic recipe, but you can use your favourite or find a recipe to suit you in any good cookery book or online. You need: 500g of strong white flour, 2 teaspoons of salt, a 7g sachet of fast-action yeast, 3 tablespoons of olive oil and 300ml of water.

Bread making is not instant and has long stretches of time when you simply have to leave the process to get on by itself. So you may like to use some of that time to think about the ingredients, letting them inform your prayers.

Begin by measuring out the flour into a large bowl. It takes little effort to open the paper packet and pour it out. But not all that long ago the work involved in that bag of flour would have been a visible part of life for many. Farmer, miller and baker were all part of the local society. The effort is hidden from most of us but is still there. People have worked at growing and harvesting the grain, milling it to flour, packaging, transporting and selling. The flour gives body, structure and flavour to the loaf. Without it there wouldn't be any bread, but by itself it is inedible. In fact, most of the ingredients that make up this loaf, with the exception of water, are of little use by themselves. In our highly individualised society and church it is good to remember that.

So, to the flour add yeast. Yeast is wonderful. So little is added in comparison to the flour, but if you forget about it, the bread is flat and hard. There have been times when I've forgotten to add it to the bread maker, and I have discovered the truth of this the hard

You may like to use some of that time to think about the ingredients, letting them inform your prayers

... little use by themselves

way! Jesus must have marvelled at the yeast's action as he watched bread being prepared. He used the action of yeast as a picture of the kingdom of God. If we are aware of struggling churches, small numbers, limited resources, it is a parable to encourage and challenge, for it is a picture of a very small amount changing a large measure of dough.

'The kingdom of heaven is like yeast that a woman took and mixed in with three measures of flour till all of it was leavened' (Matthew 13:33, NRSV).

Jesus uses yeast in a negative and warning way too. Look at Matthew 16:6 (NIV): 'Be on your guard against the yeast of the Pharisees and Sadducees.' Paul takes up the picture in 1 Corinthians 5:6–7, referring to the practice at Passover of searching out any scrap of yeast bread left in the house.

> Jesus must have marvelled at the yeast's action as he watched bread being prepared

You may like to spend some time later thinking about the two pictures of yeast. But now we need to get on with the loaf, so add the salt. Again it is a very small amount, but very important. We are used to hearing about the negative effects of too much salt in food today, but don't try to leave it out of your loaf. Besides encouraging flavour it works to control the rate of fermentation in the yeast, providing stability and a longer shelf life to the bread. Jesus calls us to function like salt in society. 'You are the salt of the earth' (Matthew 5:13). Take some time later to mull over how that works in practice today.

Now mix the flour, salt and yeast together. Make a well in the middle of the mixture and add the oil and water. The oil isn't essential, but it prevents a skin forming on the dough and helps to make the finished loaf softer. The water should be lukewarm. The yeast is a living organism, inactive when we buy it but activated by warmth and liquid to release the gas that will raise the dough. Water that is too hot will kill it; if it is too cold, it struggles to act and the bread doesn't rise as well. Cooking, especially bread making, always feels like participating in God's creative work. It is about taking ordinary, everyday ingredients and watching them turn into something special. And just as in

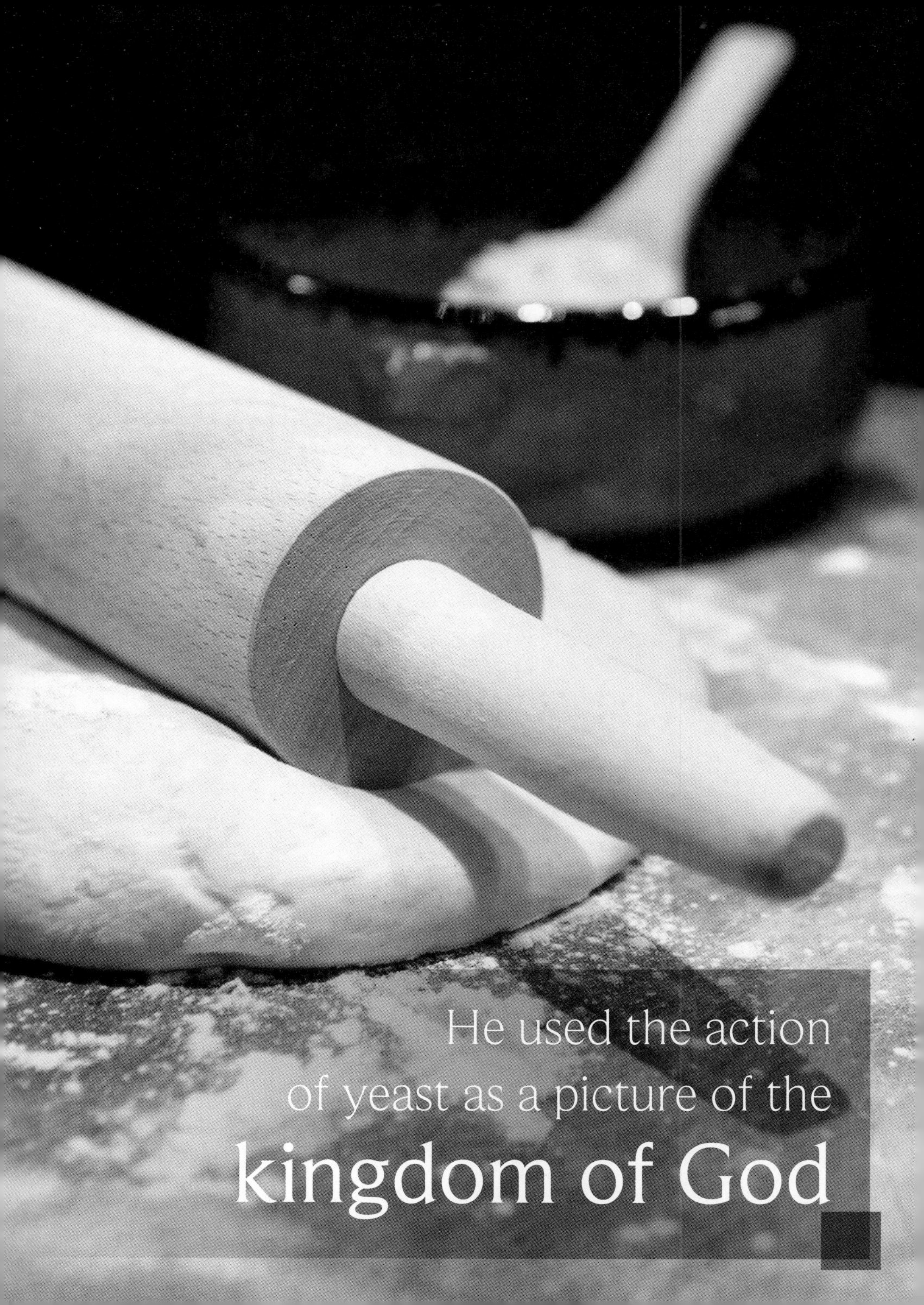
He used the action
of yeast as a picture of the
kingdom of God

Bread making always feels like participating in God's creative work. It is about taking ordinary, everyday ingredients and watching them turn into something special

the world around, the details have to be just right.

Julian of Norwich marvelled at this. 'He showed me a little thing, the size of a hazel-nut, on the palm of my hand, round like a ball. I looked at it thoughtfully and wondered, "What is this?" And the answer came, "It is all that is made." I marvelled that it continued to exist and did not suddenly disintegrate; it was so small. And again my mind supplied the answer, "It exists, both now and for ever, because God loves it"' (Julian of Norwich, *Revelations of Divine Love*, translation into modern English by Clifton Wolters, chapter 5, Penguin, 1986).

Mix everything together well, adding a couple of tablespoons more of water if the dough is too stiff, but don't make it too wet. Tip it out on to a floured surface, flour your hands, and knead. You can use the kneading hook of a food mixer. Kneading by hand is very satisfying and it feels good to get your hands into the dough. Use the heel of your hand to push the dough away from you, then fold it back on itself, give it a turn and repeat. Let yourself get into a rhythm. Keep at it until the dough feels smooth and satiny. If you press it with your finger and the indentation remains, you've done enough. Maybe turn the action into a prayer for God's shaping and kneading of your life, or say the Lord's Prayer to the rhythm of the kneading.

Place the dough in a lightly oiled bowl and leave it somewhere warm to rise for about an hour, until it has doubled in size. (You can put it in the fridge and leave it overnight. It just rises more slowly. Once, when making bread with children, we left the dough in the fridge over two nights, because of the logistics of the school timetable. It was almost leaping out of the fridge to meet us when the door was eventually opened, but the bread turned out fine in spite of everything!)

This is your time to stop, rest, think, pray, make a cup of coffee and wait. Waiting can be really difficult. We live in an instant culture and expect things to happen quickly. The Bible holds together a sense of urgency in obeying and serving God with the need to wait patiently for him to act and for him to guide. If possible, don't fill this hour with 'things that need doing', but wait, and let your waiting become a prayer.

When the dough is ready, you need to knock it back. Give it a few punches to force the air out of it. Then gently shape it into a ball and place it on a baking tray lined with cooking parchment. Now you must leave the bread to 'prove', to rise again, until it is doubled in size. Maybe this can be a resting time for you too. Go for a short walk, or put your feet up and snooze, walk round the garden, or listen to some music. Do whatever relaxes you—have some time off with God. Set the kitchen timer so that you don't have to be aware of the time.

The Bible holds together a sense of urgency in obeying and serving God **with the need to wait patiently for him...**

Now you are ready to bake the bread. Heat the oven to 200C/gas 6. Dust the loaf with a little flour and cut a cross into the top with a sharp knife. Bake it for 25–30 minutes. When the loaf sounds hollow when tapped underneath, it is ready. Cool on a wire rack—and then enjoy. Or, better still, share your newly baked bread with someone else.

THOMAS O'LOUGHLIN

The Bread of Life

Twice in the Gospel of John we meet a curious phrase where Jesus refers to himself as 'the bread of life'. 'Jesus said to them, "I am the bread of life; he who comes to me shall not hunger, and he who believes in me shall never thirst"' (John 6:35, my own translation) and then a few verses further on, 'I am the bread of life' (v. 48). The phrase is unique to these two occurrences: it is not found in the scriptures of the first generations of Christians (in our Old Testament) nor anywhere else among the other documents they themselves produced (in our New Testament). As with so many other 'I am' phrases in John (for example, 'I am the way, and the truth, and the life', 14:6), because we are familiar with them we tend to forget just how problematic they are. In the case of our two references, they have been at the heart of controversy since the later second century and debate continues today. Should they be interpreted metaphorically or directly;

author

Thomas O'Loughlin is Professor of Historical Theology in the University of Nottingham. He has published *The Didache: A Window on the Earliest Christians* (SPCK, 2010), which explores the lifestyles and beliefs of the earliest churches.

should they be seen as referring to faith in the Christ or to the Eucharist; and, since no neat system of either–or solutions 'fits' the whole context, how do we answer the residual problems any selected option throws up? This little article does not claim to have the solution, or even a solution, but rather proceeds on the premise that thinking about such phrases can attune us to listening more attentively to the Gospel.

Two preliminary observations

When we read the Gospels, we need to leave ourselves open to their enigmatic quality: we need to learn that we may never fully plumb a text's 'meaning'. This is hard for us—we like the idea that we can find out 'what it means' or 'what it meant'. This is the desire of those who want to read the Gospels as a doctrinal primer or as a collection of statements which can then be ticked off as true or false. The 'either–or' approaches that have generated more heat than light from these texts in John are symptomatic of the desire to reduce these wondrous accounts of the Christ-event to some sort of set of religious 'facts'. We should approach the Gospels more as poetry than prose, and we need to give our imagination scope to hear the evangelist whispering to us. This does not mean that we abandon academic study, but rather that we do not confuse using all our skills with the notion that what results from the use of those skills is the end of the matter. A Gospel can be analysed, but it must also be encountered. The Christian's skill lies in holding the balance: too much of one without the other can lead to learned scepticism or an idiosyncratic flight of fancy.

We should approach the Gospels more as poetry than prose, and we need to give our imagination scope to hear...

Virtually all contemporary exegetes see these phrases as being embedded as the core of a larger unit of discourse in John 6:1–72, which they call 'the bread of life discourse'. What is interesting to note here is that this unit of discourse coincides exactly with our 'chapter 6'. Such coincidences in discourse boundaries between modern and early medieval exegesis are most unusual. Our 'chapter' system (it became standardised in the twelfth century but reflects the 'headings' or *capitula* that became common in the ninth century) reflects the theological

> There are those who see Jesus as 'the Holy One of God' and can think of **nowhere else to go**

concerns of early medieval monks who had far fewer resources for the study of the Gospels and very different concerns and suppositions than we have; yet, in this case, if we try to look at what 'I am the bread of life' means within the larger context of chapter 6, we do so with a rare unanimity of theological opinion as background!

Salient points

Reading through the discourse, we see certain themes coming up again and again about who Jesus is, and there seems to be a constant 'confusion' of now/eternity, this life/heavenly life. As I read through it, I can jot down these points:

- A Passover setting
- Jesus is concerned for his followers
- A wondrous feeding
- Jesus is a prophet
- Jesus is unlimited by time and space
- Jesus is a teacher and called 'rabbi'
- Jesus gathers his hearers around him
- He talks of heavenly food
- There is a linking of now and eternity
- All comes from the Father
- There is a linking of here and heaven
- Jesus is Son of the Father
- There are links between now, the 'last day', and eternity
- Jesus has come from Joseph
- Jesus has come from heaven
- We eat his flesh
- We drink his blood
- Moses gave bread to eat
- This bread is not the same as Moses' bread
- 'Now' recalls but differs from the past in the desert
- 'Now' is not eternity but somehow links 'forward'
- People cannot appreciate this
- There is a linking of our lives, his life, and eternal life

- There is a linking of bread, heavenly bread, and eternal life
- Jesus is the 'son of man'
- There are those who walk away from Jesus
- There are those who see Jesus as 'the Holy One of God' and can think of nowhere else to go

It is worth doing a similar exercise: just jotting down what strikes you as you read through the discourse. As you do this, bear in mind that we read the text on our own, but this is a text that was intended to be heard in a group. Our reading is an individual experience that allows us to pore over the words at our own pace, and it tacitly assumes that there is the sort of logical development in the text that is inherent in any modern written piece. When we think of this as a piece of heard narrative, listened to by a group, then the repetitions, the circling backwards and forwards of ideas and the linking of one word to another become far more intelligible.

It should now be apparent that any attempt to see John 6 as the evangelist providing us with a piece of historical reportage of a couple of days' work in the life of Jesus is to miss his whole approach. Equally, it should be clear that this is not the account of a lecture by Jesus—or by the evangelist—such that we could classify it under some heading such as 'Christology', 'eschatology', 'sacramental theology' or whatever. Moreover, the either–or approaches are all inappropriate: they assume that the discourse can fit our neat categories or be seen as answering our questions. It is about who Jesus is, about now, about eternity, about the Eucharist, about judgment day, about eating, about communion with Jesus, and much, much more—and there seem to be no fences!

It is about who Jesus is, about now, about eternity, about the Eucharist, about judgment day…

A community encounter

Rather than trying to 'figure out' the text, let's try to imagine one of the communities that heard John preaching. We need to imagine quite a small group—50 would be an outside estimate—who gathered weekly on a Sunday: we can see this regular pattern of meetings reflected in John 20. (The resurrection appearance scenes in John 20 take place on Sundays: John is formulating the appearances within the liturgical paradigm of his communities' gathering which took place on Sunday.) The gathering had many aspects, but its focus was as a gathering for a meal. We should not try to impose later 'order' on this meal: it was a real meal affair, it was a time of remembering and preaching, and it was a time when the Father was blessed for what he had done in sending Jesus to his people. This blessing of the Father ('blessing' and 'thanking' are largely interchangeable words) took place in a way that recalled the table practice of Jesus, and involved the sharing of a single loaf and a common cup within the meal. We see these practices in the *Didache* and 1 Corinthians, and there are echoes elsewhere. This gathering was known by many names, including 'Eucharist' and 'agape', but we need to get over the 19th century's habit of imagining that each word referred to a separate event. There was one meal: it, *most unusually*, had men and women, Jews and Gentiles, slaves and free, rich and poor all sitting and eating together—or at least that was the aim. It was, no doubt, at times a glimpse of a new world, but at other times the petty divisions of rich/poor, nice people/

Rather than trying to 'figure out' the text, let's try to imagine one of the communities that heard John preaching

A real meal affair...

The gathering had many aspects, but its focus was as a **gathering for a meal**

© IngridHS / Shutterstock.com

smelly people, and us/'not us' re-emerged and caused divisions. We hear of the problems in 1 Corinthians and the letter of Jude. For some this was the best meal of the week; for others there were questions about why it was of any importance to gather with the rabble and eat this bread and drink this cup: what had all this eating and drinking to do with accepting Jesus as Messiah or as God's revelation? 'Unless you eat and drink…'—read John 6:53 again.

There were lots of other tensions. Christians saw themselves as the people of the renewed covenant: they were seeking the Way of Life and avoiding the Way of Death, and the key to this was the new law proclaimed by Jesus. But how did Jesus relate to the background of this new covenant, how did he relate to Moses, and was he the fulfilment of 'the scriptures' or more than these, such that they were just a preparation for him? Moses too gave bread, but how is this eating and this discipleship with Jesus to be seen in relation to that past eating and to listening to Moses? So how did the Christian faith, at the end of the first century, see itself in relation to Israel; how relevant was that past to its own understanding? How did it keep the past and move away from it?

In their everyday world there was yet another tension: the Way of the Christians involved a life of practical discipleship; it was concerned with right living and following the demands of the covenant. But it was also about life beyond this life; it spoke of salvation on the last day, and of eternal life, not here but with the Father. John holds all these tensions before us in his discourse and it was a tension each disciple had to live with. Christianity was neither a moral philosophy nor an esoteric cult, but it demanded the engagement with practical issues that characterised the former, while offering a vision of a created universe as distinctive as any of the mysteries that then grabbed attention.

> It requires the faith to see the miracle of rich and poor at one table...

Encounter

A successful 'reading' of John 6 supposes that the tensions inherent in Christian discipleship cannot be resolved into simple either–or choices or neatly wrapped up in doctrinal formulas. The various dimensions of faith have to be held in tension, while the actual encounter with Jesus takes place day by day in the events of our lives with all their clutter and confusions. This encounter with the Anointed One involves now, the past, the future, eternity. It demands moral action and community involvement. It needs both practical food and mystical nourishment. It confronts the rabbi and the prophet, but also the unique Son of the Father. It requires the faith to see the miracle of rich and poor at one table as much as the miracle of the loaves and fishes. A holistic understanding requires acknowledging the encounter with the Holy One in the memory of Jesus and in blessing the Father while sharing a loaf and a cup.

DAVID WINTER

The Bible: a heart-to-heart conversation

author

David Winter is one of the UK's most popular and long-established Christian writers and broadcasters. He has written many books, including *Facing the Darkness and Finding the Light* (BRF, 2011) and *The Road Well Travelled* (Canterbury Press, 2009).

There is a way of reading the Bible—one honoured through centuries of employment—that sees it primarily as a heart-to-heart conversation between God and the believer. Its traditional name is *lectio divina* (spiritual reading) and more and more people today are finding it a fresh and inspirational way to approach the sacred text. David Winter explains.

The Bible is an inescapable element in Christian life and worship. Every Christian service includes at least one, usually several, readings from it. Sermons, addresses and homilies pick up its themes and its message. House

> Where their own devotional life is concerned, regular reading of the scriptures sometimes seems more like a requirement or a religious chore

> It tells us how we should live our lives...

groups pore over its pages together. Many homes possess a copy, or several copies, of the Bible—and in some of them they are actually read from time to time! Sadly, however, it has to be admitted that for many Christians Bible reading is a problem rather than a blessing. They hear it read in church, but where their own devotional life is concerned, regular reading of the scriptures sometimes seems more like a requirement or a religious chore than a constant joy and inspiration.

In the second letter to Timothy there is a short list of the ways in which the scriptures can be 'useful' to us. (The scriptures referred to are of course the Hebrew Scriptures, which we call the 'Old Testament', because the New Testament didn't yet exist.) They are, the writer claims, 'useful for teaching, for reproof, for correction, and for training in righteousness, so that everyone who belongs to God may be proficient, equipped for every good work' (2 Timothy 3:16–17, NRSV).

So the Bible is 'useful'; it trains, corrects, equips. And that is probably how most of us see it: a manual of instruction, guidance, correction and encouragement. It sets out what we believe; it reveals the purposes of God; it tells us how we should live our lives and warns us of the dangers of the disobedient or rebellious life. It 'equips' us for 'good works'—it furnishes our lives with the essential elements of what we may call the godly life. The most natural way to turn to the Bible for this kind of help is to listen to sermons, to read books setting out its precepts, and to study it privately or in groups in order to uncover its message and teaching. That's how most of us have handled the Bible, in some cases alongside quite serious study of its background, culture and text. Most of us have discovered—although it may take a long while to do so—that the Bible isn't 'easy'. Its richest gold has to be painstakingly mined. Faced with that challenge, the temptation is to assume that the Bible has nothing for 'people like us' and leave it to the scholars.

The temptation is to assume that the Bible has nothing for **'people like us'**

But all through the history of the Church, disciples of Jesus have also read the Bible in a way which seems to transcend all of those approaches—or, rather, weaves them into a spiritual experience which is much greater than the sum total of their parts. It is of course vital that we read the Bible for 'information' about the faith ('teaching'). We should read it for ethical and moral warning and guidance ('reproof, correction, training in righteousness'). We should read it to equip us for God's service ('every good work').

Yet the New Testament itself recognises another way of reading the Bible and another purpose in the disciple's approach to it. Ancient tradition calls this way *lectio divina*—literally, 'divine' or spiritual reading. It makes possible a radically different, although not contradictory, approach to scripture. There's an example of it in the apostle Paul's letter to the Christians at Colosse. They are told to 'let the word of Christ dwell in you richly' (3:16). The word 'richly' here is very strong. It implies a fullness, an overflowing. Paul's hearers are to be saturated with the word of Christ—by which he presumably means the teaching of Jesus and the stories of his life, death and resurrection. That 'word' is to soak into the readers' or listeners' hearts and minds—as one person put it to me, like a rich sherry soaking down into the dull sponge at the bottom of a trifle and transforming it. There's a hint of this idea in Paul's letter to the Romans: 'the word is near you, on your lips and in your hearts' (10:8). The first letter of Peter and the letter to the Hebrews both

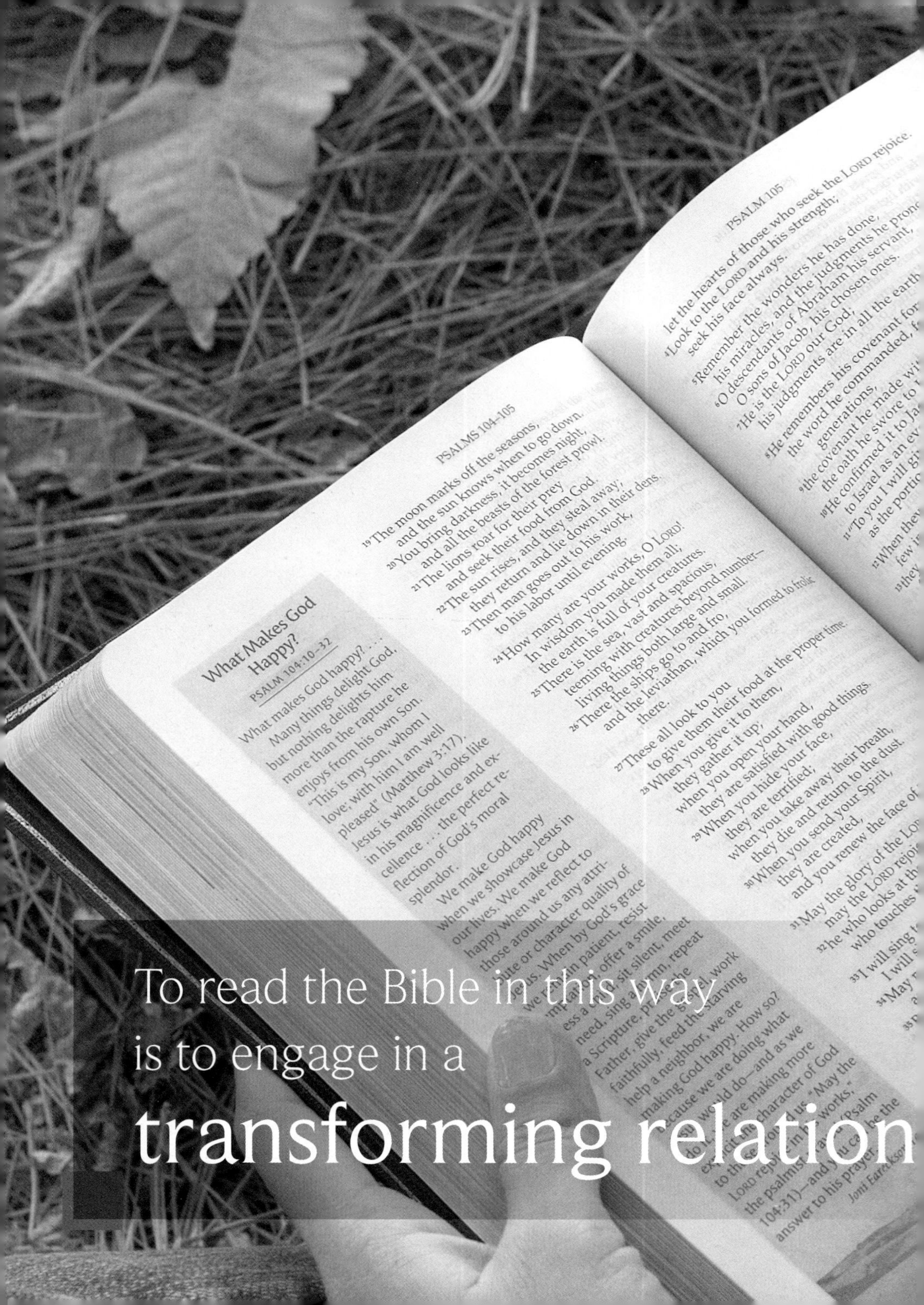

To read the Bible in this way
is to engage in a
transforming relation

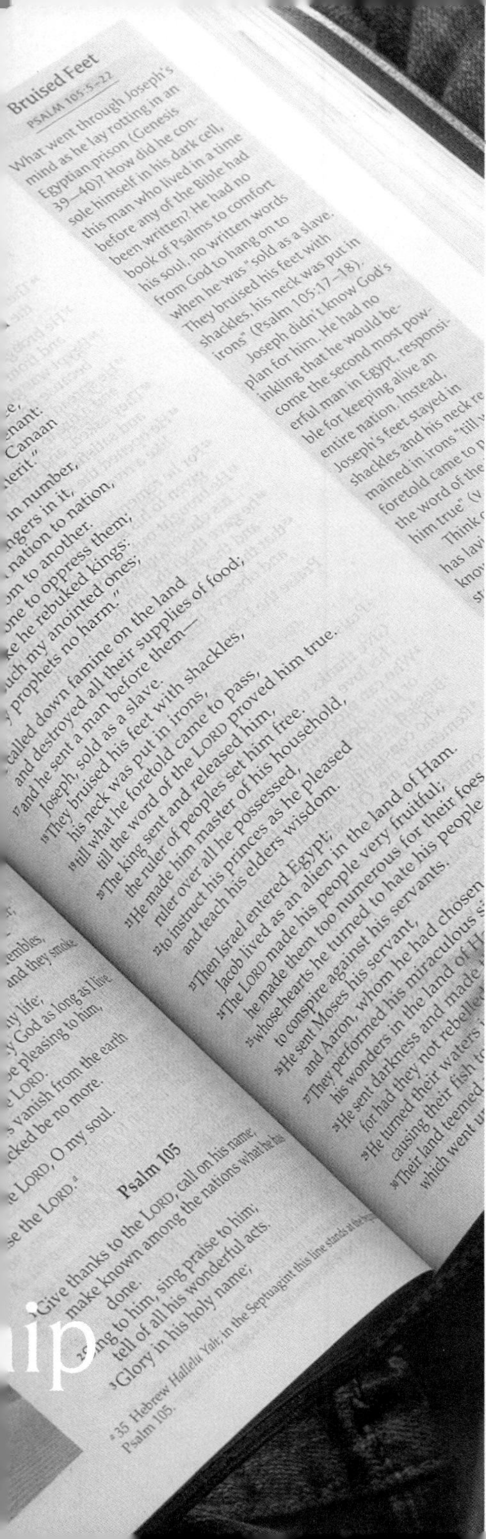

speak in the same kind of way of the word of God as 'living and active', an organism rather than a book. Indeed, we can find the same idea in the Old Testament, too: 'I treasure your word in my heart, so that I may not sin against you' (Psalm 119:11). To read the Bible in this way is to engage in a transforming relationship with the scriptures, rather than simply hearing or reading them.

However we choose to describe this way of opening ourselves to the Bible, it is much more than opening a book to find information, answers to questions, or even ethical guidance. This way is more like a conversation, an engagement with a living being, in which we open ourselves to a dynamic encounter with the divine voice which speaks through its words. It is not much concerned with questions of textual or literary analysis. It doesn't even ask the usual questions (How? When? Why? By whom?) The reader simply opens him- or herself to the scriptures in the form in which they present themselves and listens to their inner voice.

That is not at all to dismiss the value of biblical scholarship, or to say that we should never grapple with the text or use the tools of scholarly research to uncover its meaning or appreciate the particular idiom or literary form in which it is expressed. To refuse to do that is spiritual laziness or immaturity. But if painstaking study of the text is the *only* way we ever read the scriptures then we are missing much of its divine purpose. It wasn't written for the library or the lecture theatre, but to enable ordinary believers to meet with God, to hear his voice and to enter into a rich,

To use the scriptures in this particular way, we shall **need to bring certain qualities to it ourselves...**

living relationship with him, a kind of conversation of the soul.

That may all sound rather precious. In fact it is simply the 'other side' of prayer. In prayer, we think of ourselves as talking to God. In *lectio divina* we think of God as talking to us. One is, on the whole, a speaking exercise; the other is a listening one. When we turn to this kind of Bible reading, our primary responsibility is to listen—*really* listen. We open ourselves to the divine voice, keeping still and surrendered to the task. Like Elijah on Mount Horeb (1 Kings 19:11–13), our ears need to be attuned. The earthquake, the fire and the storm (the events and pressures of the day, the clamour of life) dominate. It is only when they are stilled that we can hear what the Bible calls 'the sound of sheer silence' (NRSV). You wouldn't normally expect to hear anything if all is silent. Yet in that profound silence the prophet Elijah heard the message of God, loud and clear, as we say.

To use the scriptures in this particular way, we shall need to bring certain qualities to it ourselves. We shall need attention, the focus of mind and spirit on the words before us. It requires discipline to concentrate on what we are reading and to shepherd all those wayward thoughts that would lead us away from the inner voice of the text. We shall need reflection, as we allow its message to infiltrate our thinking until it saturates our minds and wills. We may find ourselves staring at a few words for a long time, or reading and re-reading a phrase or sentence. We shall need to apply what we then hear to our own lives and circumstances, and finally we shall need to obey whatever it says to us.

It is hard to do all this if we are surrounded by various distractions, domestic or external. 'Quiet spaces' are not easily acquired commodities in modern life, and people have often told me that the absence of them is an important factor in inhibiting their own interior spiritual life. But others have found that 'those who seek, find' (see Matthew 7:7): that space is more about mental discipline than square metres, and that quietness is more than simply the absence of noise. To engage in *lectio divina*, we shall need to create that inner space and quietness, even if we live in cramped conditions and noise is more or less incessant (as it often is today). Somewhere, somehow, we shall find a place and time to hide away with the word of God and listen to his voice. It may be that, for us, the 'quiet space' is no more than a corner of precious privacy in a noisy household, or a snatched few minutes of peace while children are in the garden. It could be moments spent walking in the local park. It may even be, as one person described it to me, simply the space under the duvet at night! Whatever and wherever it is found, the time and space devoted to divine reading will be precious, because it is life-changing in its potential.

This is dynamic Bible reading, allowing the word of God to permeate our being. It doesn't require a fundamentalist view of the scriptures, simply a belief that through this text in some way (which we may not be able to define) God speaks to his people 'heart to heart'. After all, he has done it for people for thousands of years, and as they have listened he has spoken. There is time enough to encounter scripture in different ways, using it to wrestle with the profound truths of faith, or to teach and instruct us in Christian discipleship. Here, with a narrower, more intense focus, we seek from the text just one thing, but that is the greatest thing a human being can ask for: a heart-to-heart conversation with the living God.

This is dynamic Bible reading, allowing the word of God to permeate our being

TIM BLEWETT

Entertaining Angels

author

Prior to being Warden of Launde Abbey Retreat House in Leicestershire, Tim Blewett was Canon Residentiary of St Asaph Cathedral. Between these two posts he has served as Army Chaplain in Iraq to the HQ National Support Element and the Baghdad Support Unit. He is in popular demand to lead retreats and to act as a spiritual director and also to preach and teach across the country.

'Remember always to welcome strangers, for by doing this, some people have entertained angels without knowing it...'

HEBREWS 13:2 (THE NEW JERUSALEM BIBLE)

People never fail to amaze me. In this world of heightened individualism I have come across many different people in many different situations, but when I start talking to them about their lives I find that there are huge similarities despite the fact that we are told everyone is different.

People might talk about their relationships, their work, their hobbies and even their faith, but scratch a little further and you will find that people are seeking meaning, purpose and direction in their lives, whoever they

... we will realise that we are receiving far more than we will probably ever give

are and whatever they have done. In finding that meaning, that purpose, that direction, people start to find that there is a point to it all. For that process to begin, they need to be given time and space, and these are frequently in such short supply that we are not often in a position to give them. If only we could give time and space, then those we listen to would understand themselves as being of value—cared for and loved for who they are, not for what they are or what they have. Some may even be heard for the first time in their lives as we say little or nothing but truly hear what they have to say—and we may find that the strangers we welcomed into our space and into our time with compassion are indeed angels whom we are called to entertain.

This level of listening is not just listening to what is being said but hearing what is being said and what is not being said. It is taking listening deeper, to a new level—there are, after all, many people who listen but far fewer people who hear. If we can start to hear and not just listen to what is being said, then we will realise that we are receiving far more than we will probably ever give.

Sadly, though, the stranger is to be feared for many in today's world. We are taught to fear those who are unknown to us, from an early age, and to lead isolated lives where we do not make contact at any depth with others around us. If we so much as smile at

... there are huge similarities despite the fact that we are told **everyone is different**

someone we do not know, that can lead to suspicion and even fear. That fear prevents us, if we are not careful, from opening ourselves up to others. Somehow we need to allow God to transform that fear in us, that we might allow someone into our space, into our time, not just to be listened to but to be heard, to know that they are loved and valued for who they are.

Let me tell you a story.

Coming home one day, I found someone at the doorstep, a man in his thirties, who had come to do some work. He was a complete stranger to me. Over a cup of coffee the conversation opened up as he was working. He told me the story of his life—how his mother and siblings no longer spoke to him following his parents' divorce because he had not wanted to take sides, how he was seeking to find a job that provided fulfilment, and a relationship in which he could both give and receive love, how he wanted to know what it was all about. He told me how he was thinking of going to church but did not know what he would find if he did. He began as a stranger but by the time he had finished the work he was surely an angel—a messenger who had come to me to share something of his life, which changed me as I stood and listened and heard his story.

This story, which took maybe an hour to unfold, does not have to be unique if we are willing to stop and hear what is being spoken. The question is whether we are willing to do that: to stop and hear, allowing the stranger into our space.

The stranger

Over a cup of coffee the conversation opened up... he was surely an angel

is not necessarily someone we have just met: they may be someone with whom we have a relationship. They could even be our partner, a member of our family or someone we have known for years. Even the person who we believe is familiar to us might have become a stranger to us. We need to stop, listen and hear what they are saying and not saying in a way that we have not done before. In doing so we will share someone's life and we will be changed by them, no longer welcoming a stranger but entertaining an angel. We will become aware, as they will, of the many different possibilities that God lays before us as we participate in each other's lives and in the life of God within each and every one of us. By participating in such a way we mirror Christ who was caught up in those around him. If we could only follow such an approach, then many who are left on the outside of the Church, baffled by some of the doctrines to which some of those on the inside hold so dearly, would find a way forward to enter into the journey of faith.

In the simple act of welcoming someone as you listen to their story in the space they need, giving them value, the complexities of the Christian faith fall away. What counts is the person before you and whether you welcome them as if you are welcoming Christ himself. All that complicates, making faith hard, needs to be laid to one side. In that moment, as a relationship between two strangers is born, the dynamism of God's call is found. As we listen intently to the other, discerning God in them, the word of God emerges.

> ... we will share someone's life and we will be changed by them, no longer welcoming a stranger but entertaining an angel

The 'knowing' that God is present gives birth to a depth of trust as we value the person not because we 'know' everything about them but because we 'know' that they are a child of God. In that knowing, we are then called to respond to the immensity of God in them, recognising the stranger as an angel who brings a word to us and to them out of the sheer silence.

If we are to welcome strangers and entertain angels, there needs to be a realisation that we too need to be welcomed and listened to dispassionately without judgment. Without someone to do that for us, how are we are going to listen to others ourselves? If we are not willing to leave our own safe place and seek to be welcomed by another, then how can we listen to the stranger ourselves? It is only in our vulnerability that we learn from a generous host who welcomes us that God is within us. In such a meeting there is no time for the trivial or the pious posturing but rather there is a need to be real, to be honest, to be fully human. In such a way our feet are kept firmly on the ground, preventing us from becoming too spiritual.

> In that moment, as a relationship between two strangers is born, **the dynamism of God's call is found**

> As we listen intently...

When we listen to another's story unhurriedly, occasionally recognising that we need to help the storyteller tell the real story and not just the one that they present, the freedom of God is found. But to move to that real story, trust between the storyteller and the one who is listening is required. It needs to be recognised that the building of that trust can sometimes take time—it is not instantaneous. Trust cannot be rushed and there needs to be a deep waiting upon the Holy Spirit if it is to be found. In allowing the Holy Spirit (rather than ourselves) to take the central role, we can relinquish the responsibility of providing solutions and solving problems. Instead we are filled with God's grace, which is all-encompassing, and we can welcome the stranger so as to entertain angels, allowing the rubbish of today's world to be thrown away.

If we are to help the stranger, then the right questions have to be asked—the ones that go to the heart of the matter, discovering clarity and order out of the potentially chaotic. In doing so the onion layers are peeled away and truth is discovered, with the stranger being able to answer the question that Christ so often poses: 'What do you really want?' We should be prepared to ask the questions that Christ would have us ask, enabling people to hear the word of God being spoken to them and to come to an understanding that they are made in God's image, loved by him despite the fact that they have not attained to the spiritual heights people often think they should have reached.

At the heart of their search is the need to place God at the centre of all that they are: to love him with all their heart, with all their soul, and with all their mind, loving their neighbour as they love themselves. They may have other wants or needs to do with family, work or relationships but at their heart is a desire for meaning and purpose—for God. If only we can give people time and space, listening intently to them and asking the questions Christ would have us ask, we will realise that the stranger we welcomed is an angel whom we are now entertaining. We are changed by the encounter as much as they are, as God has called and we have been brought together by that calling while our relationship with each other and with God is deepened.

At the heart of their search is the need to place God at the centre of all that they are...

As the storyteller starts to bring order with God to the chaos and disorder of their lives, there is the realisation that they are loved—loved by God and united in the love of the neighbour. In discovering that they are made in God's image, that they are loved by God and by others, there is often a desire to name all those things that have been a block in their life before, to seek reconciliation with God and with their neighbour. All that we need to do, as the one who hears, is to provide that space and time,

> We have to safeguard our own journey so that we may grow in Christ **by being heard by another**

allowing the Holy Spirit to work on and in them, entertaining the angel that they are realising they are—hearing the message from God to the world.

In doing so, we, as the hearer, declare our solidarity with those to whom we listen. We recognise that we too fall short and sin just as much as anyone else and are in as much need of reconciliation as others. We are united with those we hear in our humanity and, as we listen intently with compassion, we cannot help but take their 'sins' upon ourselves as we bear the burdens of others in Christ. Just as we assure those whose stories we hear that they are both forgiven and healed by God, we too need to hear that message ourselves. As fellow human beings made in the image of God, travelling the same journey that they are, we have to safeguard our own journey so that we may grow in Christ by being heard by another.

In giving space and time, compassionately hearing those around us, we are called to stretch out beyond the boundaries that are surrounding us: to touch and be touched by those on the margins. All people want to be heard, so that they might not always be strangers but might be angels—messengers of God. It should not just be limited to the formal encounter, as we should be open to all people, in our work and in our leisure, ready to hear others. This is costly but ultimately we are given more by those we hear than we give to them, as we see them flourish while the Christ in them grows and they become more fully who they are called to be. All we need to give is time and space and to hear with compassion, that in welcoming strangers we might entertain angels.

My Space

This space is for you to make your own notes.

A lovely new loaf just waiting to be cut and eaten

© Harris Shiffman/Shutterstock.com

TONY HORSFALL

Tony's reflections: The best meal of the day

author

Tony Horsfall is a freelance trainer and retreat leader living in Yorkshire. He is the author of *Mentoring for Spiritual Growth* (BRF, 2008) and *Working from a Place of Rest* (BRF, 2010)—see www.brfonline.org.uk for further information.

It is often said that breakfast is the most important meal of the day. Children preparing for a hard day at school, and busy parents going to work or looking after the family, need to begin the day with the right 'fuel' to keep them going. Some people, surprisingly, skip breakfast, but not me—it's my favourite meal!

In the Christian life it's also important to begin the day well, and for many believers that means time alone with God. Of course we can connect with God at any time, but it seems sensible to me to meet with God before rushing off into the day's activities. This appears

It is often said that breakfast is the most important meal of the day

to have been the pattern for Jesus (Mark 1:35), and comes highly recommended by the psalmist (for example, Psalm 5:3; 59:16; 88:13).

As a young Christian I was brought up to have a regular 'Quiet Time', and it remains for me a helpful spiritual practice. How can we ensure that it doesn't become a dull routine, something we do because we 'must'?

> The most commonly found ingredients are **scripture, prayer and worship**

Here are four important keys:

- ❖ Rhythm—life works best when there is a regular pattern, and making time each morning to meet with God is a good habit to adopt. It doesn't matter if you miss occasionally, but generally try to keep to the pattern. A rhythm makes it easier.
- ❖ Variety—it is the spice of life, and varying what we do in our time apart can keep it fresh and alive. Review your Quiet Time often. Be creative and imaginative.
- ❖ Place—create a special place where you can meet with God. A quiet corner of the house, a comfy armchair, a room with a view... make it 'sacred', perhaps with a small table for books, your coffee cup, a small cross or icon and so on. For some it may be outdoors: a special walk you take with the dog, a church you drop into on your way to work, a bench in the park.
- ❖ Purpose—keep in mind why you are doing this: to meet with God in a life-giving way. Aim to enjoy his company, express your dependency upon him as you begin your day and seek his will for your life. Don't let any particular activity become dominant; you are there to meet with God.

With these four provisos in our minds, what then will occupy us during our Quiet Time? The most commonly found ingredients are scripture, prayer and worship.

Scripture

The word of God is at the heart of the devotional life, providing sustenance for our souls. Jesus said: 'Man does not live on bread alone, but on every word that comes from the mouth of God' (Deuteronomy 8:3; Matthew 4:4, NIV). We need to develop effective ways to absorb the truths of scripture.

Some people follow a reading programme or lectionary, leading them through the whole Bible in a year or two in daily portions. Others enjoy developing plans of their own—reading steadily through different books of the Bible, following themes or topics, looking at Bible characters. A good number have Bible reading notes to guide them, or commentaries to provide understanding.

Sometimes I enjoy reading the Bible imaginatively, in the way of Ignatius, where we are encouraged to place ourselves into the Bible story and see it through the eyes of those involved. Another approach I enjoy is called contemplative Bible reading (*lectio divina*), where we read a short passage slowly and allow a word of phrase to speak to us, receiving it as God's word to us for that moment and meditating on it (see David Winter's article on pages 19–25).

The important thing is to try new ways of interacting with scripture and not to become stale. Many resources are available on the Internet, and for downloading as well. See for example: Quiet Time Ministries (www.qtmin.com), Crossmap Daily Quiet Time (http://dailyqt.crossmap.com) and BRF's own Bible reading notes available as printed copies, as PDFs and for iPhone (www.brfonline.org.uk/daily-bible-reading).

Prayer

If scripture provides food for the soul, then prayer supplies us with oxygen. It is the way by which we commune with God, our core purpose when establishing a Quiet Time. Whatever else we do, we should reach out to God with longing and desire, speaking freely and honestly to the lover of our souls.

> The word of God is at the heart of the devotional life, providing sustenance for our souls

Some people are happy speaking to God in their own words (aloud or silent), while others enjoy the objectivity of Spirit-inspired and Christ-centred liturgy, joining the stream of prayer down the centuries. Most enjoy a mixture. I often base my prayers on the Lord's Prayer, using each phrase in turn as a 'coat hanger' on which to hang other prayers. Occasionally I have done the same with Psalm 23 and the 'armour passage' in Ephesians 6:10–18. A framework like this stops my mind from wandering.

I love using the great prayers of the Bible too, and making them my own. Currently I am finding satisfaction in crafting my own prayers—taking the passage from my daily reading and turning my thoughts into a prayer that I write down.

Some days we may have no words at all, which is fine; enjoy the silence, be still and know that he is God—a true quiet time!

Use your senses to encounter the living God in the world around you

Worship

Worship connects us to the Holy Spirit and is the way we drink the living water to satisfy our thirsty souls. By taking time to give thanks to God for his goodness, we cultivate a grateful heart; by dwelling on his greatness and glory we allow faith to grow within us. Worship enables us to express our love for God, and as we give to him our praise and adoration, his grace and strength come streaming back to us, preparing us for all that lies ahead.

We have a family friend, over a hundred years old now, whose constant companion throughout her life has been the Methodist hymn book, a source of great blessing and encouragement to her. The words of hymns and songs have a wonderful capacity to lift our spirits, to reach us when our souls are dry and barren.

We can listen meditatively to music as we sit, walk or drive and even as we do our chores, and our spirits can be in communion with God; or we can open our lungs in full-blown praise! Allow the glory of creation to inspire you as you get out and about. Use your senses to encounter the living God in the world around you; be inspired by works of art, objects of beauty, the wonders of the animal kingdom.

Remember, there is no right or wrong way to have a Quiet Time, and it should never be regarded as a burden or impossible demand. Hold it lightly, and yet think of it as the main spiritual meal of your day. And then, fortified and nourished by the grace of God, go out and live for Jesus in our needy world!

Margaret's Space

Margaret Harvey is a retired priest in the Church in Wales. She has been running Coleg y Groes Retreat House. Margaret writes a regular column in *Quiet Spaces*.

> It is a wonderful story of an experience of **God's care, provision and guidance...**

'For the journey'. It's the annoying by-line of an advertisement currently on TV that has us joining in with it every time it appears on the screen. It has made me realise how often the word 'journey' is being used. Have you noticed? Participants in reality TV shows, interviews, competitions and documentaries all talk about 'the journey' that they have been on. Overuse can cause an idea to become more or less meaningless. This would be a pity, as the image of journeying is a very powerful one in the Bible. Maybe we need to reclaim it.

Try doing a Bible search for the

use of 'journey' and the related word 'way'. You can use an Internet site, such as www.biblegateway.com, or a good concordance, or just start reading through the Bible looking out for journeys. This last method will take longer but will be very rewarding.

Here are some gems you will meet on the way.

In Genesis 24, Abraham sends his servant on a journey to find a wife for his son, Isaac. It is a wonderful story of an experience of God's care, provision and guidance. I love the King James translation of verse 27: 'I being in the way, the Lord led me.' It sums up our role, to 'be in the way', and affirms God's faithfulness in travelling along with us.

The Old Testament has a journey at its heart. Exodus tells the story of the emergent people of Israel journeying from slavery to freedom. Try reading the whole book in a modern translation rather than picking out short passages. Notice the ups and downs, the excitements and the long times spent just travelling on, and let it resonate with your own journey.

Journeys can lead to new life and transformation (as with Paul in Acts 9). The encounters with the people we meet can be life-changing and sometimes we will be used by God to change things too (as with the Ethiopian official and Philip in Acts 8:26–40).

So, enjoy exploring journeys. And remember you need provisions. This issue is about that food.

Notice the ups and downs, the excitements and the long times spent just travelling on, and **let it resonate with your own journey**

And remember you need provisions...

'Bread Time' Liturgy

Some organisations have hit on the idea of asking people to give a certain amount of money over a period of time on every occasion when they do a particular thing. This can go on for anything from a week to the whole of Lent, as far as I can see. So here is a shorter idea you may like to use with a group on a Quiet Day. First of all, decide the cause to which you would like the money to be given. Maybe most appropriate would be an organisation that promotes the production or study of the Bible. Below are some suggestions about amounts you may suggest people give, but you would need to tailor the amounts according to the probable make-up of the group. For example, if all the members are pensioners on a fixed income, you could decide on the amounts suggested below, but if you think people may be able to afford it, you could invite them to give more.

... promotes the production or study of the Bible

Let us be still before God

You may find it helpful to copy out this list beforehand, or make another quite different list, but if you are using this liturgy you will need six different amounts in this order:

- ❖ 10p if you prefer white bread or 5p if you prefer brown
- ❖ 50p if you have a bread making machine
- ❖ 5p for every shop where you regularly buy bread
- ❖ 5p for every sandwich you eat today—remembering those who have no food
- ❖ 20p for every loaf or part loaf you have at home at the moment
- ❖ 10p for every slice of bread or toast you have eaten today

When you have decided and written this down, tell the people concerned so that they can find enough change to bring with them on the day. It would probably be better to give a copy of the list to each person before you start, and allow them to work out what they will need, to avoid having to do some mental arithmetic during the time together!

Meanwhile, place a loaf and a candle on a low table in the middle of the group. Have a bowl for collecting the money. This could be on the table if people would like to get up and put their money in it, or maybe it would be sensible to have a smaller bowl that could be passed around. The money could be put into this before being transferred into the large bowl on the table at the end of each section of the liturgy below. (This would avoid the small one getting too heavy with small change and making it difficult to pass between people.)

You should also tell people before starting, 'When I say "Lord in your mercy", we say together "Hear our prayer"', and it may be best to do this immediately so that people are familiar with it.

Leader: Let us be still before God... Into the silence we bring our thanks. Thanks for our daily bread. As we look at the loaf so we give thanks for the people who bought this, that they had both the money and the opportunity to do so. They could choose to buy brown or white, sliced or uncut, everyday or special. We pray, Lord, for those who have no choices to make today because of their poverty, and for those who are now facing starvation.

Leave a quiet space in which people can put the money into the container.

Lord, in your mercy, **hear our prayer.**

Allow silence for a short time.

Leader: Into the silence we bring our thanks for all we have. Some have machines at home to make their own bread. We have cookers and microwaves to produce hot food. We pray for those in the developing world who lack tools, or flour, or a place to make bread. We pray for those who live in regions ruined by drought, flooding or warfare.

Leave a quiet space in which people can put the money into the container.

Lord, in your mercy, **hear our prayer**.

Allow silence for a short time.

Leader: Into the silence we bring our locality; the places where we live. We pray for this place/these places. For all who work here/there, especially those in the shops which serve our need, and where we buy our daily bread. Help us to value place and people; those whom we meet as well as those who farm or work in factories where food is prepared.

Leave a quiet space in which people can put the money into the container.

Lord, in your mercy, **hear our prayer**.

Allow silence for a short time.

Leader: Into the silence we bring our thanksgiving for our senses. Today we will eat bread. We will taste it, smell it, enjoy it. We thank God for our senses, especially for the senses of taste and smell, essentials in our appreciation of bread. Help us to use our senses well in the appreciation of your creation. Help us to see the wonder of all your creation, even in the things we consider to be everyday items, which we can so easily take for granted.

Leave a quiet space in which people can put the money into the container.

Lord, in your mercy, **hear our prayer**.

Allow silence for a short time.

Leader: Into the silence we bring our thanksgiving for the family of faith to which we belong. We thank you for making us part of your family, the body of Christ. So we celebrate Christ's coming into the world, his birth at

Bethlehem, 'the house of bread', his proclamation of himself as the 'bread of life', his death on the cross and his glorious resurrection. Help us to follow in his footsteps, pointing to him as the one who offers the bread of life to the world.

Leave a quiet space in which people can put the money into the container.

Lord, in your mercy, **hear our prayer**.

Allow silence for a short time.

Leader: Into the silence we bring our need of Jesus, the bread of life. Help us to be partakers of him, that we may never hunger or thirst, but walk in the strength of his life within us, receiving his gifts of bread and wine in the company of his people throughout all time and eternity.

Leave a quiet space in which people can put the money into the container.

Lord, in your mercy, **hear our prayer**.

Allow silence for a short time.

Leader: Let us finish our time together by saying the Christian family prayer, **'Our Father...'**

Into the silence we bring our thanksgiving for our senses. Today we will eat bread

You may like to ask people to stop after the phrase 'give us today our daily bread' for a couple of minutes, continuing again afterwards with 'Forgive us our trespasses...'

You could close your time together by saying the grace, or you may like to say or sing the psalm found on page 59 of this issue of Quiet Spaces.

HEATHER FENTON

Bethlehem: house of bread

> We meet all sorts of characters in the Gospel

I have long been fascinated by the way in which the story of Jesus is so involved with places. We meet all sorts of characters in the Gospel narratives, and very often they are put into a geographical context. Looking at the early part of Jesus' ministry, for example, John writes about the call of Philip. John says, 'Philip, like Andrew and Peter, was from the town of Bethsaida' (John 1:44, NIV). Philip goes to find Nathanael saying: 'We have found the one Moses wrote about in the Law, and about whom the prophets also wrote—Jesus of Nazareth, the son of Joseph' (v. 45). Nathanael is clearly very sceptical about all this, replying, 'Nazareth! Can anything good come from there?' (v. 46). It is not a good place to come from, he feels!

Jesus is, in typical rural style, described by the place from which he is perceived to have come. Just as we have 'John Bryn Gwynt' (John of Windy Hill) in Wales, so we have 'Jesus of Nazareth'. But this Jesus could also have

author

Heather Fenton works as a parish priest and an editor.

been called 'Jesus of Bethlehem', and indeed this may have made him more recognisable to some!

The Bethlehem that was to welcome the Son of God was no stranger to biblical visitors. It appears in the Old Testament on a number of occasions, and was known variously as Ephrath (Genesis 35:16), Bethlehem Ephrathah (Micah 5:2), Bethlehem in Judah (1 Samuel 17:12), and in the New Testament is named as 'the town of David' (Luke 2:4). In Hebrew *Beit Lehem* literally translates as 'house of bread'. So in itself Bethlehem is therefore a notable place and its name both anticipates and reflects the nature of its most famous child.

But note that Philip says to Nathanael that they have found the one whom Moses wrote about in the Law and about whom the prophets wrote; this 'Jesus of Nazareth' (or 'Jesus of Bethlehem') is a really significant person. He turns out to be not only from the 'house of bread', but to be in himself the house of bread; the bread of life (John 6:48–51)!

The chief priests and the teachers of the law came up with the **right answer...**

He is the one to whom the Old Testament prophets look forward. In Hebrews 11 the writer talks about those who had looked forward 'by faith'. Hebrews 11, after listing a few characters who looked forward in faith says: 'All these people were still living by faith when they died. They did not receive the things promised; they only saw them and welcomed them from a distance' (v. 13, NIV). That promise was Jesus, foreseen but not fully revealed.

There are many prophecies about Jesus in the Old Testament. One that we read every Christmas comes from Micah 5:2: 'But you, Bethlehem Ephrathah, though you are small amongst the clans of Judah, out of you will come for me one who will be ruler of Israel, whose origins are from of old, from ancient times'. So the person who comes from Bethlehem is 'from of old, from ancient times' and this is again presented to us in another reading we sometimes associate with Christmas, this time from the prologue of John's Gospel: 'He was with God in the beginning' (1:2). In Matthew's account of the coming of the wise men, they

> The feeding of the 5000 is a story that is included in all four Gospels, which probably means that all four authors saw it as having special significance

No beginning or end...

look for the newborn child and ask for information about the whereabouts of this special birth to which they had been guided by a star. The chief priests and the teachers of the law come up with the right answer: 'In Bethlehem in Judea' (Matthew 2:5), they tell Herod. This child clearly belongs in Bethlehem; Luke shows us that Joseph is from 'the house and line of David' (2:4). The 'wise men', foreigners who come to Bethlehem, the house of bread, are also foretold as outsiders—'the kings of Tarshish and of distant shores will bring tribute to him; the kings of Sheba and Seba will present him gifts' (Psalm 72:10). The prophet Isaiah speaks of the special glorious light of the Lord thus: 'Nations will come to your light, and kings to the brightness of your dawn' (Isaiah 60:3).

The feeding of the 5000 is a story that is included in all four Gospels, which probably means that all four authors saw it as having special significance. In John's Gospel (6:1–14) this is shortly followed by Jesus' teaching that he himself is 'the bread of life' (v. 35). We are drawn into a deeper understanding of Exodus 16:4. In John 6:32–33 Jesus says, 'I tell you the truth, it is not Moses who has given you the bread from heaven, but it is my Father who gives the true bread from heaven. For the bread of God is he who comes down from heaven, and gives life to the world.' Again, here is the man from the house of bread. And he goes on to say, 'I am the living bread!' (v. 51) and 'Whoever eats my flesh and drinks my blood has eternal life' (v. 54). Some of his listeners do not like this, and in answering them Jesus declares, 'For my flesh is real food and my blood is real drink' (v. 55).

Way back in the Old Testament we see a 'type' or mystical foreshadowing of Christ. In Genesis 14 Melchizedek, King of Salem (the place later to be known as Jerusalem), comes bearing bread and wine (v. 18). In the same verse, he is described as 'priest of God Most High', the one to whom Abraham gave a tenth of everything. He is also one who has no beginning or end, and the writer of the letter to the Hebrews picks this up and reflects on the connection between Jesus and Melchizedek (6:20—7:21). He is worthy of receiving an offering from Abraham, marking him out as superior; he appears in some sense to be outside time; and he comes bearing bread and wine as well as being King of Salem.

So let us go back to what I said about the importance of Jesus and place in the Gospel narratives. It seems to me that where God has given a particular blessing to a place, there sometimes follows great trauma. The most outstanding examples in the context of Jesus' life are the city of Jerusalem and the 'little town of Bethlehem'. This little town, visited by angels, shepherds and kings, the birth place of the 'bread of life', is now traumatised by the circumstances and, indeed, the wall which surrounds it. So let us, with the psalmist, 'pray for the peace of Jerusalem' (Psalm 122:6) and its near neighbour, Bethlehem 'the house of bread'—that little place which held the bread basket of the world.

He is worthy of receiving an offering from Abraham, marking him out as superior; he appears in some sense to be outside time...

You may find the following website interesting: www.breadonthewaters.com/0025_Prophecies_Concerning_Jesus_Christ.html.

JOHN BIRCH

John's Prayers

author

John Birch is a Methodist Lay Preacher and worship leader and has been living in Wales for around 20 years. He is also a regular contributor to the International Bible Reading Fellowship notes, and his prayers have appeared on various websites. You can find more material on his website (see below).

Somewhere
a miracle occurs,
a seed is sown
in fertile ground,
germinates,
grows, ripens
and in due season
will be harvested.

Somewhere
a miracle occurs,
from the simplest
of ingredients,
flour and water,
salt and yeast,
kneaded and formed.
Daily bread.

Somewhere
a miracle occurs,
your word is sown
in fertile ground,
germinates,
grows, fruits
and in due season
will be harvested.

Somewhere
a miracle occurs,
as the purest
of ingredients,

love, hope
and joy make
broken lives whole.
Bread of Life.

God of miracle,
provider of
daily bread,
word of life
and love,
we offer you
our thanks.

Bread of Life, you feed us
through word and sacrament.
The bread we share
a remembrance
of your presence with us.
Strengthen us for service,
that seeds we sow
in fertile places
might grow and flourish,
that food we share
in fellowship
might nourish and revive,
that words we share
in our daily walk
might glorify your name.
Bread of Life, you feed us
through word and sacrament
that we might feed others.
Blessed be your name!

When the journey is long
and we hunger and thirst,
Bread of Life, you sustain us.
When the road is hard
and our bodies weak
Bread of Life, you heal us.
When our spirits are low
and we can't carry on
Bread of Life, you revive us.
When we offer our hand
in love and in service
Bread of life, you bless us.
When the challenge is great
and the workers are few
Bread of Life, you empower us.
When the victory is won
and we see your face
Bread of Life, you will rejoice with us!

We bless you,
God of Seed and Harvest
Provider of our daily bread
And we bless each other
That the beauty of this world
And the love that created it
Might be expressed though our lives
And be a blessing to others
Now and always.

WWW.FAITHANDWORSHIP.COM

My Space

This space is for you to make your own notes.

A lovely new loaf just waiting to be cut and eaten

HEATHER FENTON

'Give us this day our daily bread'

> These days there is usually a considerable choice of bread in our supermarkets...

author

Heather Fenton works as a parish priest and an editor.

'Give us this day our daily bread,' we confidently pray regularly, without connecting with what that might mean. These days there is usually a considerable choice of bread in our supermarkets and even in our village shop, unless you arrive too late in the afternoon, and there is at least the possibility of sliced or unsliced, brown or white bread. These days too, even if we miss out on being able to buy any bread made for us, we may have a bread machine and the quick cook programme sometimes comes in very useful! So bread is something we tend

to think of as readily obtainable.

Those of you old enough to remember the Second World War can probably remember the national loaf, the 'take it or leave it' option. Younger people, who may be especially conscious about how we need to live in a more environmentally aware way in our world, may have already begun to notice articles in the press about the problems of producing wheat flour as a result of climate change. Times are changing yet again and maybe we will be back to having a more cautious view of the unquestioning availability of our 'daily bread'. It is good that we look at how people approached the idea of daily bread in the past, in the hope that we can learn from them. So read on!

I will never forget going to St Beuno's, Pistyll, on the Lleyn Peninsular in North Wales where Lammastide is still taken seriously. This ancient little church, set in a hollow near the sea, has no electricity and the floor is strewn with rushes at Lammastide as well as at Christmas and Easter. I

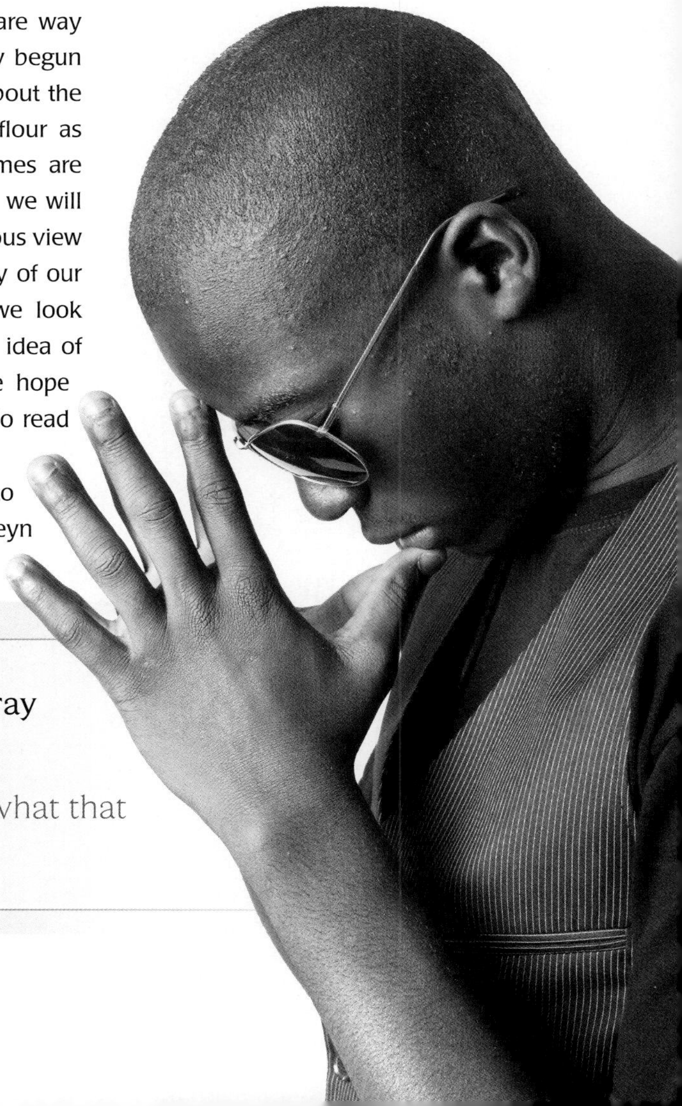

We confidently pray regularly, without connecting with what that might mean

remember coming in from the daylight, and walking into the dark interior with its sweet-smelling rushes. Here was a glimpse of a world where some of our certainties about, among other things, bread, would not fit easily. It made me want to discover more.

Here was a glimpse of a world where some of our certainties about, among other things, bread, would not fit easily. It made me want to discover more

Lammas day is on 1 August. The word 'lammas' first appears in the writing of King Alfred and may come from an old English word for loaf, followed by 'Mass'. In medieval times it was also known as 'Gule of August', possibly an English pronunciation of the Welsh *Gwyl Aust*, which translates literally as August festival. It was the custom to consecrate bread, made from the first ripe corn, on that day.

In Bible times, too, for most people having enough bread would have always been a major concern. Praying 'give us this day our daily bread' was such an obvious and basic thing for Jesus to include in the prayer he taught his disciples (see Matthew 6:11 and Luke 11:3), even if we subconsciously reinterpret it today as 'give us this day the things we need', which is probably more than basic sustenance in our complicated world. Jesus mentions this again when he says, 'Do not worry about your life, what you will eat or drink; or about your body, what you will wear. Is not life more important than food, and the body more important than clothes?' (Matthew 6:25, NIV).

The boy with the five barley loaves and two fish at the feeding of the 5000 had what was probably the most common form of bread. Wheat was the best flour, and sometimes spelt was used. Whatever grain was available, it would have been sorted in a shallow basket, and tares (poisonous seeds such as darnel) would have been removed (see the parable of the weeds and the seeds in Matthew 13:24–30, 36–43). Jesus also used another bread image to talk of the kingdom of God: in Matthew 13:33 he says, 'The kingdom of heaven is like yeast that a woman took and mixed into a large amount of flour' (probably about 22 litres) 'until it worked all through the dough'. The flour was mixed with water or sometimes olive oil. Fresh yeast was seldom available, so a piece of fermented dough or leaven from a previous baking was kneaded into the new dough and left to rise (see also the reference to the yeast of the Pharisees: 'Be on your guard against the yeast of the Pharisees and Sadducees', Matthew 16:6). After rising, part of it was put aside for the next day's baking, as this flat bread was appetising when fresh but soon went dry and could not be kept for long.

Obtaining the grain was a laborious process. In the early summer, the harvests of barley and wheat would be cut with sickles and bundled into sheaves. These were loaded on to donkeys or carts and taken to the 'threshing floor', a site usually held in common between all the inhabitants of a village. Threshing was usually done by beating with a stick, and then the grain was 'winnowed' by tossing it into the air, which made the straw blow to one side while the heavier grain fell on to the floor. The grain had to be stored in a dry, rodent-proof place until it was needed.

> **Praying 'give us this day our daily bread'** was such an obvious and basic thing for Jesus to include in the prayer he taught his disciples...

In the Old Testament, in their

wilderness wanderings, the people of God were fed by him with manna (see Exodus 16) and eventually, when their nomadic life ceased and they lived a settled existence that meant they could engage in farming, God instructed his people about celebrating harvest: 'When you have entered the land that the Lord your God is giving you as an inheritance and have taken possession of it and settled in it, take some of the firstfruits of all that you produce from the soil of the land that the Lord your God is giving you and put them in a basket. Then go to the place that the Lord your God will choose as a dwelling for his Name and say to the priest in office at the time, "I declare today to the Lord your God that I have come to the land that the Lord swore to our forefathers to give us"' (Deuteronomy 26:1–3). They were not to forget that God was the source of the provision of all that they needed for their life.

When their nomadic life ceased and they lived a settled existence that meant they could engage in farming, **God instructed his people about celebrating harvest**

A basic staple of most people's diets...

It may be a basic staple of most people's diets in the West even today, but it is good for us to remember that we should not take our daily bread for granted. You could try planning a celebration of Lammastide later on in the year. This could include using Psalm 65 and maybe also trying to make some soda farls (see the recipe on pages 60–61).

Psalm 65 can be used to celebrate God's provision of the harvest. The tune to which these words go is 'The Ash Grove'.

1. *We praise you, our God, and we pay*
our vows to you,
For you are the one who responds
when we pray.
To you shall all flesh come to make
their confession,
When sins overwhelm us you purge
them away.
With blessings you satisfy us in your
temple,
How happy are those whom you
choose and bring near.
With dread deeds you answer, Oh God
our Salvation,
Through all the wide earth, God, our
help and our stay.

2. *In your strength you set fast the*
earth's mighty mountains,
You still the sea's raging, the roaring
of waves;
And clamorous peoples fall silent and
tremble,
The gates of the morning and night
sing your praise.
You visit the earth and you water and
tend it,
With grain in abundance your people
are fed.
With showers you soften the ground
and prepare it,
You water its furrows and smooth out
its ways.

In your strength
you set fast the earth's
mighty mountains,
You still the sea's raging,
the roaring of waves;

3. *And so every year's richly crowned*
with your goodness
Your paths overflow with your
bounty and love,
The wild places flow with the streams
of your bounty
And joy forms a girdle round
mountains above;
The flocks on the hillside, so many in
number,
The meadows are dressed in a
garment of sheep;
Ripe corn clothes the valleys, they
shout with delight and
Together they praise you and sing of
your love.

Why not make some Irish soda bread farls?

> Make the dough into a flattened circle about half an inch thick and cut it into quarters...

If you are having a quiet day, by yourself or with some other people, you could make some bread farls. These are traditionally made in the northern areas of Ireland. They are made with soda bread dough, which is flattened into a circle, and divided into four parts—the meaning of the Gaelic word 'fardel'. They are then cooked on a dry griddle or frying pan. They are best eaten warm.

To make them you will need two cups of plain flour, one teaspoon of baking soda, one cup of buttermilk and a pinch of salt. You need to sieve the flour and baking soda into a bowl, and then make a well in the middle into which you gradually add the buttermilk. Work them in together, working quickly and lightly to mix the dough and then tip it out on to a well-floured surface and knead lightly. Make the dough into a flattened circle about half an inch thick and cut it into quarters with a floured knife.

Preheat the griddle and check the temperature by dusting with a small amount of flour. Once it starts to colour, your griddle or pan is at the right heat. Brush off the flour and turn the heat down. Your pan or griddle is now ready. Once you have a good colour on one side of the farls (which will be after about 2–3 minutes), turn them over and cook for a further 5–10 minutes. You can test to see if they are ready by pressing the middle. If they are still 'squidgy' you can turn them again for a few minutes. They can be cooled on a rack and eaten as soon as possible! Jam and maybe cream would be good, although they go well with bacon too.

Preheat the griddle and check the temperature

Jesus Christ the apple tree

Under the shadow...

The tree of life my soul hath seen,
Laden with fruit and always green:
The trees of nature fruitless be
Compared with Christ the apple tree.

His beauty doth all things excel:
By faith I know, but ne'er can tell,
The glory which I now can see
In Jesus Christ the apple tree.

For happiness I long have sought,
And pleasure dearly I have bought:
I missed of all; but now I see
'Tis found in Christ the apple tree.

I'm weary with my former toil,
Here I will sit and rest a while:
Under the shadow I will be,
Of Jesus Christ the apple tree.

This fruit doth make my soul to thrive,
It keeps my dying faith alive:
Which makes my soul in haste to be
With Jesus Christ the apple tree.

This poem was written by an unknown person in New England, a place where apple trees commonly grow. It was first published in 1784 in a book called *Divine Hymns or Spiritual Songs*. It is thought that the song may be an allusion to the description of the apple tree in the Song of Songs (2:3). It has been set to music a number of times.

Looking at the world through the eyes of Alexander Carmichael

Alexander Carmichael was someone who was very interested in ancient Celtic folk material. He was born in 1832 in Taylochan on the Isle of Lismore. His was the oldest family in the area and this gave him a special interest in the past. In 1864 his work took him to the Uists, and he discovered that this area was particularly rich in historical material. He soon became well known for his desire to talk to people who were still able to recite the ancient stories, hymns, poems, riddles and observations. The material he collected became the basis of a collection we know as the *Carmina Gadelica*, the first volume of which was

> This area was particularly rich in historical material

published in 1900. It reflects a deeply agricultural society in which every detail of daily life could and should be brought to God. Here is an example of a prayer for milking time, and another about reaping the harvest. (In the latter, 'Bride' and 'Columba' are two Celtic saints, both Irish in origin. This was another common feature of remote western areas where there was a sense that these people were still part of the community.)

Forgetting God amid the ordinary details of our daily life, for that is that they were, is not good...

Maybe we can find ways of thanking God for bread

Bless, O God, my little cow,
Bless, O God, my desire;
Bless thou my partnership
And the milking of my hands, O God.

Bless, O God, each teat,
Bless, O Lord, each finger;
Bless thou each drop
That goes into my pitcher, O God!

Here is another prayer poem, this time about reaping:

God bless thou thyself my reaping,
Every ridge and plain and field,
Every sickle curved, shapely hard,
Each ear and handful in the sheaf,
Each ear and handful in the sheaf.

Bless each maiden and youth
Each woman and each tender youngling,
Safeguard them beneath thy shield of strength,
And guard them in the house of the saints,
Guard them in the house of the saints.

Encompass each goat, sheep and lamb,
Each cow and horse and store,
Surround thou the flocks and herds,
And tend them to a kindly fold,
Tend them to a kindly fold.

For the sake of Michael head of hosts,
Of Mary fair-skinned branch of grace,
Of Bride smooth white of ringleted locks,
Of Columba of the graves and tombs,
Columba of the graves and tombs.

The last item I shall quote from the *Carmina Gadelica* is about 'smooring', that is banking up the peat fire so that it smoulders gently through the night:

The sacred Three,
To save
To shield,
To surround
The hearth,
The house,
The household,
This eve,
This night,
Oh! this eve
This night
And every single night
Each single night!

Well, you and I may not have cows to milk, a harvest to reap or even a fire to bank up. But what these and other contributions in the *Carmina Gadelica* show us is that taking things for granted and forgetting God amid the ordinary details of our daily life, for that is what they were, is not good. Maybe we can find ways of thanking God for bread as we put it in the toaster and for milk as we take that awkward top off the plastic container, as well as when we begin our bedtime routine. And I am sure, if we look for them, we will also see plenty of other opportunities in what we know as the ordinary rhythms of our days to pray, to thank God for what, for us, is the ordinary pattern of our living.

© monbibi / Shutterstock.com

ELENA BOSETTI

Meditating with Scripture: John's Gospel

author

Elena Bosetti teaches New Testament at the Gregorian University in Rome and also the Institute of Religious Studies in Modena. She is the author of many popular books on scripture and is a Sister of Jesus the Good Shepherd of the Pauline Family.

This is an extract from *Meditating with Scripture: John's Gospel* (BRF, 2010) by Elena Bosetti, who helps us to think about the idea of *lectio divina*, which we started to think about in the article by David Winter. For further information about the book, see www.brfonline.org.uk.

The great prayer of Jesus

With no precise topographical setting, but ideally placed at the summit of the farewell address and as a 'bridge' between the upper room and Gethsemane, Jesus' great prayer to the Father, also called 'the priestly prayer', stands out in John 17. Everything Jesus said to and shared with his disciples in the context of the Last Supper (see John 13–16) is gathered, as it were, in this prayerful ascent from the Son to the Father.

The entrance into this prayer is indicated, even before the words begin, with body language and, more specifically, with a gaze: Jesus 'lifted his eyes to Heaven' (v. 1), as though to establish a direct contact with the Father, to whom he entrusts his own destiny and that of his followers. To lift one's eyes to heaven is a biblical gesture that characterises a person at prayer: 'To you I lift up my eyes, O you who are enthroned in the heavens!' (Psalm 123:1). Jesus teaches us to pray with these words, 'Our Father Who art in Heaven' (Matthew 6:9–13).

> He does not seek glory from human beings, but only the **glory that comes from God**

Let us ask the Holy Spirit to bring us into this great prayer. Let us ask Jesus to help us enter into his own sentiments in total mutual exchange with the Father and in the indescribable joy that flows from his filial relationship. Lord Jesus, help us feel your love for the Church and make us participants in your passion for unity.

A glance at the structure

Various elements of form and content converge to highlight the structure of John 17, which opens with an introduction (vv. 1–5) in which Jesus asks the Father to glorify him. A central part follows, which is divided into three sections: first, a retrospective look at the mission already carried out (vv. 6–10); second, a request to the Father to guard and consecrate his own in the truth (vv. 11–19); third, a broadened view into a universal prayer that embraces future believers and asks that 'all may be one' (vv. 20–23). Finally, there is a conclusion, where the theme of glory/glorification returns, a theme that Jesus wishes to share with his disciples (vv. 24–26).

Jesus knows that his hour is approaching, the hour of suffering and death, and with immense trust he asks the Father first of all to glorify him. He does not seek glory from human beings, but only the glory that comes from God. He asks the Father to make the glory of his love fully resplendent. The request for glorification implies the resurrection of Jesus, the indispensable condition for fulfilling the supreme mission he received from the Father—that of communicating eternal life to all humanity.

Jesus presents the Father with four requests. Three of these are formulated with imperative verbs: 'glorify' (your Son); 'guard' (or 'keep' those you have given me); 'consecrate' them in the truth. The fourth request is formulated with the verb *erotao*, 'I pray', and has as its object unity: 'that all may be one!'

> He entrusts his own future and that of his community to the Father...

The articulation of this passage highlights a double perspective: behind and ahead. After the introduction, we note above all a retrospective view of the mission carried out. It is a gaze full of gratitude that admits having received everything from the Father. The insistence on gift and reciprocity is striking. For Jesus, too—as is typical in the Bible—prayer is above all a remembering. The hour has arrived. The present is charged with a fullness, that of the mission accomplished. It is charged with Jesus' joy at having accomplished the work for which the Father sent him into the world. But Jesus also looks ahead; he looks to the future. He entrusts his own future and that of his community to the Father. He prays that all may be one, as he and the Father are one. Jesus speaks as though he is no longer with his own, as though he has already left the world. There is a play on the words 'presence' and 'absence'. The conclusion refers back to the introduction: Jesus prays again for his own glorification and for ours, and he prays for the Church's unity.

Elena then takes us on to look at this passage in detail, helping us to understand some of the keywords which Jesus uses before going on to encourage us to reread the passage as a whole whilst pausing to contemplate the 'various scenes which compose this sublime prayer'. She then invites us to enter into a dialogue with Jesus.

Dialoguing with the Word

Let us enter into dialogue with Jesus, making his prayer our own. The first Christians lived the exciting experience of meeting God as the trustworthy Father of Jesus Christ. In the letters of Paul and Peter, we find three hymns of benediction that begin with the same words: 'Blessed be the God and Father of our Lord Jesus Christ' (2 Corinthians 1:3; Ephesians 1:3; 1 Peter 1:3).

How do I live in filial relationship with the Father? What does being sons and daughters of the Father imply? Am I grateful for all God continually offers and gives me?

Jesus lives in joy because he lives in love, in full communion with the Father and with his own people. Joy flows from love and must be shared in order to be total. Jesus desires that this same joy might dwell in us, that nothing will disturb this joy, that no one will take it away from us. He desires that heaven may already exist here and now: in our hearts filled with his joy!

'They were Yours and You gave them to me,' Jesus said. We, too, can say this about our loved ones, especially our brothers and sisters in faith. Community is given to us as a gift even before it is a commitment and call to responsibility. Do I live my fraternal relationships as a gift?

How do I embrace Jesus' prayer for unity? How much do I let my heart be touched by his passion for unity? Does his ardent desire burn in me: 'that all may be one'? How do I participate in bringing about this divine project?

> It is a gaze full of gratitude that admits having received everything from the Father

> He looks to the future...

MARTYN PAYNE

The People's Bible

The People's Bible is published by BRF as a practical guide for primary school teachers but has some material from which adults can learn too! The following is an extract from this book. In writing this, the author, Martyn Payne, has made clear the effects of having the Bible published in one's own mother tongue. As we take for granted the availability of the Bible in many translations and formats today, it is an eye-opener to reflect on the consequences of this in 1611.

author

Martyn Payne is a member of the Barnabas children's ministry team and the author of several books, including *Footsteps to the Feast* (BRF, 2007) and *The Big Story* (BRF, 2011).

The publication of the King James Version in 1611 meant that the words of the Bible were now available to everyone in the contemporary English of the day. The People's Bible had exploded on to the world! Its publication set in motion a chain of events that would change individuals, communities, nations and even, in time, the whole world.

Although there had already been English translations available before this, particularly in the previous hundred years, nevertheless the officially approved, regally sanctioned and state-promoted King James (Authorised) Version opened the floodgates. Now anybody anywhere could hear and understand the stories of the Christians' special book, and this turned everything upside down.

Already, in the 16th century, the Bible in English had ignited change. It had helped people to see that they didn't need the church or the king to tell them what to believe. Now that lots of people had the opportunity to read this book, or hear it read, in their own language, they also discovered that kings can sometimes be wrong. So when they got a king who thought he couldn't do anything wrong because God had made him king, there were bound to be consequences. In the 17th century, more and more people asked questions like 'Who should really be in charge?' and 'Do we even need a king?' Unfortunately, King Charles I didn't really understand what was going on. He believed in the 'divine right of kings' to do exactly what he wanted, and disagreements with Parliament about this finally led to the English Civil War in 1642. Although the king believed that the Bible supported his position, it provided plenty of ammunition for his enemies, who started by questioning his actions and, in the end, cut off his head. Biblical ideas had changed the way people saw the world.

> They also discovered that kings can sometimes be wrong...

Having the Bible available for individuals and groups to read also opened up new understandings of scripture. They read, for example, that Jesus never founded 'a church' as such and that his first followers wrote about 'the priesthood of all believers'. Church power did not need, it seemed, to reside in the hands of a few trained professionals; anyone could be inspired by God's Spirit to lead and guide a congregation. So new denominations sprang up, organising themselves on these spiritual and democratic principles. They objected to the existing structures of the Church of England and were therefore called 'dissenters'. The state church clamped down on these believers, so many of them decided to seek a new life and to start a Christian utopia in the New World. In 1621 some of them set out westward in a ship called the *Mayflower* and became the founding fathers of the State of America; this was, to a large degree, because the Bible could now be read by all in English.

Other groups were formed with different understandings of baptism, about the need for bishops to govern the church, and about the ways in which the Holy Spirit inspired worship. For example, in the middle of the 17th century, the Society of Friends was founded, also called Quakers, who read for themselves in the Bible about God's passion for justice in society and how all people everywhere should be treated with respect and dignity. As a result, many of them stood up against unfair practices in business and against laws that disadvantaged the poor and the weak in society.

> They discovered that Jesus had chosen the ordinary workmen of his day to be disciples

Others found themselves questioning the received understandings of some Christian doctrines, and so were moved to study the scriptures again for themselves. It was while doing just this that the brothers Charles and John Wesley came to a new understanding of how much God loved them, and this filled them with joy and a passion to share their faith. They took their message out on to the streets and into the countryside of Great Britain, preaching the good news of the gospel to ordinary workers. They set up small classes everywhere, in which the new converts could study the scriptures for themselves. So it was that the Methodist Church was formed. Charles and John Wesley also took the words they read in the Bible and turned them into poetry, setting the words to the popular tunes of the day. Some historians say that this revival, during the 18th century, prevented England from falling into the despair of revolution that gripped the rest of Europe at this time. Again, all this happened because the Bible was available in the people's language.

Enslaved Africans, such as Samuel Sharpe and Olaudah Equiano, read in the Bible about the equality of all people before God, and were empowered to begin their own personal campaigns to abolish the slave trade. Biblical ideas informed Quaker opposition to the trade, and later influenced notable researchers and campaigners, such as Thomas Clarkson and then William Wilberforce, who forced the debate in Parliament. After many years, the abolition of slavery in the British Empire was finally achieved against entrenched political and financial opposition—but the world's first 'popular' political campaign had been fuelled by a biblical idea that continues to affect the whole world.

It was also because Christians could now read the Bible for themselves that they discovered that Jesus had chosen the ordinary workmen of his day to be disciples. Missionary work was not, it seemed, just for professional monks or clergyman. Anyone could be called, and so, during the 18th and 19th centuries, an army of people set sail to take the gospel 'to the ends of the earth'. It was in this period that many missionary societies were formed. It was because these people now read their Bibles that they wanted to take its story to other nations. With the Bible, they also brought health care and education, and a passion to help the poor and disadvantaged in every society in obedience to what they had read.

These stories might seem light years away from today's world, where, although Bibles are freely available, they are often left unread. However, the big ideas like those found in the Bible can spread among people like a fire spreading through a forest, as long as the conditions are right. The Bible is packed with big ideas waiting to be found, and every few years a new one breaks out. One of the latest big ideas has been the 'Drop the Debt' campaign, which protests about the injustice of poorer countries owing such huge amounts of money to the richer ones that they are impossible to pay back. This comes directly from the 'Year of Jubilee' idea found in the Bible in Leviticus 25:8–17.

> All this happened because the Bible was available in the people's language

article

RACHEL BOULDING AND DR ALISON SHELL

Celebrating the King James Version

Celebrating the King James Version is written by Rachel Boulding and published by BRF. Rachel asked Dr Alison Shell to write an Afterword, explaining the literary and historical value of the King James Version, and this extract of the afterword helps us to see the historical context and the longer-term consequences of the publication of what we know as the King James Version.

authors

Rachel Boulding is Deputy Editor of the Church Times.

Dr Alison Shell teaches in the English Department of University College, London.

The making of the King James Bible

The translators involved on all these projects were inspired by the most up-to-date scholarly standards of the age, which involved checking several manuscripts against each other and trying to establish which readings were the earliest and most authoritative.

Thus there was a massive body of previous expertise to draw on when the team responsible for the King James Bible began their work. Even so, theirs was an impressive achievement: the project was accomplished in a very short time (eight years) and with immense managerial effectiveness. Forty-seven scholars were involved in translating, and each translator's work had to be scrutinised by a group, while two individuals from each of the three centres of translation—Westminster, Oxford and Cambridge—were responsible for overseeing the complete text and preparing it for publication. A careful balance was struck between unity and diversity (each team member was neither to go out on a limb from the others nor to impose a misleading uniformity) and experts in various languages were consulted.

Being able to draw on so many different types of expertise lent the project huge intellectual authority, at a time when the Church of England, beset by Catholics on one side and Puritan separatists on the other, especially needed to show its strength. But the epithet 'Authorised Version', by which the King James Bible is also known, refers to the royal backing that was just as crucial to its status.

One of James VI and I's first acts, when he succeeded to the combined thrones of England and Scotland in 1603, had been to call a meeting with his bishops to discuss the possibility of a new translation that reflected his hierarchical notions of Church and

The translators involved on all these projects were inspired by the most **up-to-date scholarly standards of the age**

Theirs was an impressive achievement

state. At a politically sensitive time, the Geneva Bible's downplaying of a king's role and government by bishops demanded robust counteraction.

Other reasons, too, make it appropriate that James should be permanently associated with this version of scripture. As perhaps the most theologically literate monarch that England has ever had, he saw his headship of the Church of England as an opportunity to educate his people and bring about greater understanding between the religious factions of his time.

This ecumenical aim could only have been helped by the translators' debt to the Protestant pioneers of an earlier generation. This is a debt that comes over in thousands of echoes, making the experience of reading the King James Bible one of hearing many voices.

> A profound effect on the English language and the national imagination

The team was operating at a fortunate historical moment, benefiting from previous translators' good ideas but able to refine them. But this respect for past scholars also had an effect on the style of the King James Bible, at a time when the English language was changing at enormous speed. Much of its vocabulary and syntax would have come across as old-fashioned, even to its first audiences, and 400 years later many passages now need translation themselves.

Yet this unfamiliarity has also enhanced the aesthetic experience that the King James Bible offers, instilling a sense of awe in its hearers and helping to define what we think of as high style. Remarkably, for most of its history, its elevated language has not limited its accessibility. From the time of its publication, it has had a profound effect on the English language and the national imagination at all social levels, from the educated to those who were unable to read it but heard it read out loud.

The King James Bible and popular culture

Designed from the first to be heard as well as perused, the King James Bible became more widely familiar than any other text, through being read aloud in church and within household worship.

Learning and Christianity went hand in hand

For generations of Englishmen who had received only an elementary education, learning and Christianity went hand in hand. As the best prose model they were likely to encounter, it taught them both a faith and a literary style.

The Pilgrim's Progress, written by the self-taught John Bunyan, remains one of English literature's most sustained attempts to imitate biblical narrative, while its more introspective moments remind us of the powerful influence biblical poetry has had on Christian self-examination. When the hero Christian meets a man in an iron cage and asks how he came to be in this condition, the man's reply is patterned like a psalm: 'I left off to watch, and be sober; I laid the reins upon the neck of my lusts; I sinned against the light of the word, and the goodness of God; I have grieved the Spirit, and he is gone…'

For the illiterate and barely literate, the King James Bible provided a storehouse of metaphor and proverbial wisdom, as shown by the rustic characters in the novels of Thomas Hardy (1840–1928). Concerned that the rural culture he knew as a boy was dying off, Hardy had a historian's interest in recording peasants' language and thought patterns, while deploying them as only a sophisticated creative writer could.

In the final passage of *Far from the Madding Crowd*, for instance, Joseph Poorgrass's comment on the wedding of Gabriel Oak to the *femme fatale* Bathsheba Everdene strikes a note of foreboding: 'I wish him joy o' her; though I were once or twice upon saying today with holy Hosea, in my scripture manner, "Ephraim is joined to idols: let him alone"' (Hosea 4:17).

... an opportunity to educate his people and bring about greater understanding between the religious factions of his time

Inspiration for literature

'The Bible as literature'

From its first appearance, the King James Bible would also have informed the work and worship of those who benefited from a university education. But the study of the Bible from a purely literary point of view came later in the day, as English literature and the English language made their way into the university curriculum in the 19th century.

The literary importance of the King James Bible gave it a claim to be studied alongside classical literature as a source and inspiration for literature written in the English tongue; but, for many from the mid-Victorian era to the present day, Judaism and Christianity deserved no more respect than the religions of ancient Greece and Rome.

It is significant that Percy Bysshe Shelley (1792–1822), notorious in the early 19th century as a scoffer at established religion, was one of the first to distinguish literary and devotional modes of reading the Bible. His fellow poet Lord Byron (1788–1824) described him as a 'great admirer of scripture as a composition', a suggestive anticipation of the phrase familiar to us now, 'the Bible as literature'. In the present day, as secularism and religious diversity have led to unfamiliarity with the Bible, teaching it as an aid to understanding Britain's literary heritage has become more essential than ever.

As if to bear out the prediction of the Victorian commentator Matthew Arnold (1822–88) that literature would come to fulfil some of the needs previously met by religion, the growth of agnosticism and atheism as respectable intellectual options has, if anything, confirmed the literary eminence of the King James Version.

Translators of religious texts have often recognised the difficulties inherent in reconciling truth and literary elegance—a tension that can be seen in English writers from the Wycliffites onwards—and it has proved possible for many latter-day readers to discount the truth claims of the King James Bible while continuing to enjoy its narrative drive, quotability and evocations of transcendence.

The notion that several books of the Old Testament are best read as legendary—scandalous to the Victorians, standard to most today—has contributed to this development, as has the view that human creativity can be seen as a way of working alongside God rather than in opposition to him. Most Christians now would see nothing wrong with the idea of acknowledging the Bible's literary merit and power to inspire imaginative writers.

Secularism and religious diversity have led to unfamiliarity with the Bible

Even so, creative responses to the King James Bible have led in some highly original directions, even in earlier centuries, and even among those who would not have questioned that the Bible was the word of God.

Quiet Spaces subscriptions

Quiet Spaces is published three times a year, in May, September and January. To take out a subscription, please complete this form, indicating the month in which you would like your subscription to begin.

❑ I would like to take out a subscription myself

Name ____________________

Address ____________________

Postcode __________ Telephone Number ____________________

Email ____________________

❑ Please do not send me further information about BRF publications.

❑ I would like to give a gift subscription (please complete your name and address above and details of the person you want to give a subscription to below)

Gift subscription name ____________________

Gift subscription address ____________________

____

____________________ Postcode __________

Please send beginning with the May 11 / Sep 11 / Jan 12 issue: (delete as applicable)

(please tick box)	UK	SURFACE	AIRMAIL
Quiet Spaces	❑ £16.95	❑ £19.05	❑ £21.60

Please complete the payment details below and send this coupon, with payment to: BRF, 15 The Chambers, Vineyard, Abingdon OX14 3FE.

Method: ❑ Cheque (payable to BRF) ❑ Mastercard ❑ Visa ❑ Maestro

Card no. ☐☐☐☐☐☐☐☐☐☐☐☐☐☐☐☐☐☐☐

Valid from ☐☐☐☐ Expires ☐☐☐☐ Issue no. of Maestro card ☐☐☐

Security Code ☐☐☐

Signature ____________________ Date ____/____/____

All orders must be accompanied by the appropriate payment.

BRF is a Registered Charity

PROMO REF: QSBREAD

To order *Quiet Spaces* or other BRF publications mentioned in this journal, visit your local Christian bookshop or go to BRF's website www.brfonline.org.uk.